**200+ Frequently Asked Inte.**
**Testing**

**99% Asked Interview Q & A**

**(Selenium and Cucumber Testing Tools)**

By Bandana Ojha

## Introduction

This book contains 200+ frequently asked Interview Q & A in Selenium automation testing and will cover Q & A on different testing framework using Selenium WebDriver, TestNG, Selenium Page Object Models, Selenium WebDriver for browser testing, Selenium RC, Selenium IDE, Xpath, Selenium Components, Continues Integration, Selenium Extension, Exceptions, JUnits, Annotations, Selenium Accessors, Cucumber testing tool and many more.

The author of this book conducted so many interviews at various companies and meticulously collected all the important and frequently asked interview questions and answers with simple, straightforward explanations. Rather than going through comprehensive, textbook-sized reference guides, this book includes only the information required immediately to start his/her career as an automated tester. Answers of all the questions are short and to the point. We assure that you will get here the 99% frequently asked interview questions and answers.

**Good luck to ALL!!!**

## 1. What is Automation Testing?

Automation testing is the process of testing a software or application using an automation testing tool. Automation testing involves the use of a separate testing tool which lets you create test scripts that can be executed repeatedly and doesn't require any manual intervention.

## 2. What are the benefits of Automation Testing?

Benefits of Automation testing are:

Supports execution of repeated test cases

Aids in testing a large test matrix

Enables parallel execution

Encourages unattended execution

Improves accuracy thereby reducing human generated errors

Saves time and money

## 3. What is a Framework?

Framework is a constructive blend of various guidelines, coding standards, concepts, processes, practices, project hierarchies, modularity, reporting mechanism, test data injections to perform an automation testing.

## 4. What are the advantage of test automation framework?

Below are the advantages of test automation framework-

Reusability of code

Maximum coverage

Recovery scenario

Low-cost maintenance

Minimal manual intervention

Easy Reporting

## 5. What are most common Testing Framework?

There are different types of automation frameworks and the most common types are:

Data Driven Testing Framework

Keyword Driven Testing Framework

Hybrid Testing Framework

## 6. What is data driven automated testing?

Data driven automated testing is a method in which the test data set is created in the excel sheet and then imported into automation testing tools to feed to the software under test.

## 7. What is a data driven framework?

In this framework, the test data is separated and kept outside the test scripts, while test case logic resides in test scripts.  Test data is read from the external files (Excel Files) and are loaded into the variables inside the test script.  Variables are used for both for input values and for verification values.

## 8. What are the Pros of data driven framework?

The most important feature of this framework is that it considerably reduces the total number of scripts required to cover all the possible combinations of test scenarios. Thus, lesser amount of code is required to test a complete set of scenarios.

Any change in the test data matrix would not hamper the test script code.

Increases flexibility and maintainability

A single test scenario can be executed altering the test data values

## 9. What are the cons of data driven framework?

The process is complex and requires an extra effort to come up with the test data sources and reading mechanism.

Requires proficiency in a programming language that is being used to develop test scripts.

## 10. What is Keyword Driven Testing?

Keyword-driven testing is a type of functional automation testing which is also known as table-driven testing or action word-based testing. In Keyword-driven testing, we use a table format, usually a spreadsheet, to define keywords or action words for each function that we would like to execute.

## 11. What is a keyword driven framework?

The keyword driven frameworks require the development of data tables and keywords, independent of the test automation. In a keyword driven test, the functionality of the application under test is documented in a table as well as step by step instructions for each test.

### 12.What is the Pros of keyword driven framework?

In addition to advantages provided by Data Driven testing, the Keyword driven framework doesn't require the user to possess scripting knowledge, unlike Data Driven Testing.

A single keyword can be used across multiple test scripts.

### 13. What is the Cons of keyword driven framework?

The user should be well versed with the Keyword creation mechanism to be able to efficiently leverage the benefits provided by the framework.

The framework becomes complicated gradually as it grows, and several new keywords are introduced.

### 14. What is a hybrid framework?

A hybrid framework is a combination of one or more frameworks. It is associated with combination of data driven and keyword driven frameworks where both the test data and test actions are kept in external files in the form of table.

### 15. What is module-based testing framework?

Module based testing framework divides the entire "Application Under Test" into several logical and isolated modules. For each module, a separate and independent test script is created. Thus, when these test scripts took together builds a larger test script representing more than one module.

These modules are separated by an abstraction layer in such a way that the changes made in the sections of the application doesn't yield effects on this module.

### 16. What is the pros of module-based testing framework?

The framework introduces the high level of modularization which leads to easier and cost-efficient maintenance.

The framework is pretty much scalable

If the changes are implemented in one part of the application, only the test script representing that part of the application needs to be fixed to leave all the other parts untouched

### 17. What is the cons of module-based testing framework?

While implementing test scripts for each module separately, we embed the test data (Data with which we are supposed to perform testing) into the test scripts. Thus, whenever we are supposed to test with a different set of test data, it requires the manipulations to be made in the test scripts.

### 18. What is Selenium?

Selenium is an open source, browser based automated testing tool to test web applications. It supports different platforms, languages and browsers.

### 19. What are the advantages of Selenium?

Following are the advantages of Selenium:

-Free and open source

-Have large user base and helping communities

-Have cross-browser compatibility

- Have great platform compatibility (Windows, Mac OS, Linux etc.)

-Supports multiple programming languages (Java, C#, Ruby, Python, Pearl etc.)

-Has fresh and regular repository developments

-Supports distributed testing

## 20. What are the limitations of Selenium?

Following are the limitations of Selenium:

1.Selenium supports testing of only web-based applications

2.Mobile applications cannot be tested using Selenium

3.Captcha and Bar code readers cannot be tested using Selenium

4.Reports can only be generated using third party tools like TestNG or Junit.

5.As Selenium is a free tool, thus there is no ready vendor support though the user can find numerous helping communities.

6.User is expected to possess prior programming language knowledge.

### 21. What is Selenium grid?

Selenium Grid is a part of the Selenium Suite that specializes in running multiple tests across different browsers, operating systems, and machines in parallel.

### 22. What are the advantages of Selenium Grid?

It allows running test cases in parallel thereby saving test execution time.

It allows multi-browser testing

It allows us to execute test cases on multi-platform

### 23. What is a hub in Selenium Grid?

A hub is a server or a central point that controls the test executions on different machines.

### 24. What is a node in Selenium Grid?

Node is the machine which is attached to the hub. There can be multiple nodes in Selenium Grid.

### 25. What are the types of WebDriver available in Selenium?

The different drivers available in selenium are:

Firefox Driver

Internet Explorer Driver

Chrome Driver

Safari Driver

Opera Driver

Android Driver

iPhone Driver

Html Unit Driver

## 26. What is Selenium IDE?

Selenium IDE (Integrated Development Environment) is a Firefox plugin used to record and playback the test scripts. Even though we can create scripts using Selenium IDE, we need to use Selenium RC or Selenium WebDriver to write more advanced and robust test cases.

## 27. What are the advantages of selenium IDE?

Below are the advantages of selenium IDE

Recorded script converts into different components and languages.

Default object identification.

Can run test suites periodically.

Record and playback.

Create test cases.

Create test suites.

We can debug test cases.

We can edit test cases

## 28.What are the disadvantage in IDE?

Below are the disadvantages in IDE:

It Only supports Firefox.

It supports only page operations.

Limitations in Automation.

It does not support enhance test cases.

We can't store elements.

## 29. What is selenium RC (Remote Control)?

Selenium IDE have limitations in terms of browser support and language support. By using Selenium RC limitation can be diminished.

On different platforms and different web browser for automating web application selenium RC is used with languages like Java, C#, Perl, Python

Selenium RC is a java based and using any language it can interact with the web application

Using server, you can bypass the restriction and run your automation script running against any web application

## 30. Why Selenium RC is used?

Selenium IDE does not directly support many functions like condition statements, Iteration, logging and reporting of test results, unexpected error handling and so on as IDE supports only HTML language. To handle such issues Selenium RC is used it supports the language like Perl, Ruby, Python, PHP using these languages we can write the program to achieve the IDE issues.

## 31. What are the advantages of selenium RC?

Below are the advantages of selenium RC

-It supports multiple languages.

-It supports different environment.

-It supports multiple browser.

### 32. What is the main difference between web-driver and RC?

The main difference between Selenium RC and Webdriver is that, selenium RC injects javascript function into browsers when the page is loaded. On the other hand, Selenium Webdriver drives the browser using browsers built in support

### 33. What are the frameworks available in RC?

A collection of libraries and classes is known as Framework and they are helpful when a tester has to automate test cases.

NUnit, JUnit, TestNG, Bromine, RSpec, unittest are some of the frameworks available in RC .

### 34. How can to handle pop-ups in RC ?

To handle pop-ups in RC using selectWindow method, pop-up window is selected and windowFocus method will give the control from current window to pop-up windows and perform actions according to script.

### 35. What are the limitations while using Selenium RC?

Apart from "same origin policy" restriction from js, Selenium is also restricted from exercising anything that is outside browser.

## 36. Can we use Selenium RC to drive tests on two different browsers on one operating system without Selenium Grid?

Yes, it is possible when you are not using JAVA testing framework. Instead of using Java testing framework if you are using java client driver of selenium then TestNG allows you to do this. By using "parallel=test" attribute you can set tests to be executed in parallel and can define two different tests, each using different browser.

## 37. Why to use TestNG with Selenium RC?

If you want full automation against different server and client platforms, you need a way to invoke the tests from a command line process, reports that tells you what happened and flexibility in how you create your test suites. TestNG gives that flexibility.

## 38. What is Object Repository in Selenium WebDriver?

Object Repository is used to store element locator values in a centralized location instead of hard coding them within the scripts. We do create a property file (.properties) to store all the element locators and these property files act as an object repository in Selenium WebDriver.

## 39. How you build Object Repository in your project?

In Selenium, there is no default Object Repository concept. It doesn't mean that there is no Object Repository in Selenium. Even though there is no default one still we could create our own. In Selenium, we call objects as locators (such as ID, Name, Class Name, Tag Name, Link

Text, Partial Link Text, XPath, and CSS). Object repository is a collection of objects. One of the ways to create Object Repository is to place all the locators in a separate file (i.e., properties file). But the best way is to use Page Object Model. In the Page Object Model Design Pattern, each web page is represented as a class. All the objects related to a page of a web application are stored in a class.

**40. What is Page Object Model or POM?**

Page Object Model is a Design Pattern which has become popular in Selenium Test Automation. It is widely used design pattern in Selenium for enhancing test maintenance and reducing code duplication. Page object model (POM) can be used in any kind of framework such as modular, data-driven, keyword driven, hybrid framework etc.  A page object is an object-oriented class that serves as an interface to a page of your Application Under Test (AUT). The tests then use the methods of this page object class whenever they need to interact with the User Interface (UI) of that page. The benefit is that if the UI changes for the page, the tests themselves don't need to change, only the code within the page object needs to change. Subsequently, all changes to support that new UI is in one place.

**41. What are the advantages of POM?**

The advantages are POM are-

Using POM, we can create an Object Repository, a set of web elements in separate files along with their associated functions. Thereby keeping code clean.

For any change in UI (or web elements) only page object files are required to be updated leaving test files unchanged.

It makes code reusable and maintainable.

## 42. What is Page Factory?

We have seen that 'Page Object Model' is a way of representing an application in a test framework. For every 'page' in the application, we create a Page Object to reference the 'page' whereas a 'Page Factory' is one way of implementing the 'Page Object Model'.

## 43. What is the difference between Page Object Model (POM) and Page Factory?

Page Object is a class that represents a web page and hold the functionality and members.

Page Factory is a way to initialize the web elements you want to interact with within the page object when you create an instance of it.

## 44. What are the advantages of Page Object Model Framework?

Code reusability – We could achieve code reusability by writing the code once and use it in different tests.

Code maintainability – There is a clean separation between test code and page specific code such as locators and layout which becomes very easy to maintain code. Code changes only on Page Object Classes when a UI change occurs. It enhances test maintenance and reduces code duplication.

Object Repository – Each page will be defined as a java class. All the fields in the page will be defined in an interface as members. The class will then implement the interface.

Readability – Improves readability due to clean separation between test code and page specific code

## 45. What is TestNG?

TestNG is a testing framework based on JUnit and NUnit to simplify a broad range of testing needs, from unit testing to integration testing.

## 46. List out some of the functionality in TestNG which makes it more effective?

The functionality which makes it efficient testing framework are:

Support for annotations

Support for data-driven testing

Flexible test configuration

Ability to re-execute failed test cases

Excellent result generation compare to junit.

Easy way to execute a test case from suite files.

Can generate user define crystal reports.

Parameter can be defined from suite file.

Without the main method also, we can execute our script.

## 47. What is TestNG listeners and why it is used?

A listener is defined as an interface that modifies the default TestNG's behavior. As a name suggests Listeners "listen" to the event of defined in the selenium script and behave accordingly. TestNG is used in a selenium by implementing Listeners Interface. It allows customizing TestNG reports or logs. Widely used Listener is ITestListener

### 48. What is the use of @Factory annotation in TestNG?

@Factory annotation helps in dynamic execution of test cases. Using @Factory annotation we can pass parameters to the whole test class at run time. The parameters passed can be used by one or more test methods of that class.

### 49. How can we create data driven framework using testNG?

Using @DataProvider we can create a data driven framework in which data is passed to the associated test method and multiple iteration of the test runs for the different test data values passed from the @DataProvider method. The method annotated with @DataProvider annotation return a 2D array of object.

### 50. How to disable a test method in TestNG?

To disable the test method, we have to use enabled = false to the @Test annotation.

@Test(enabled = false)

### 51. How to ignore/exclude a test method in TestNG?

To ignore/exclude the test method, we have to use enabled = false to the @Test annotation. @Test(enabled = false)

### 52. How to Terminate the test method in TestNG?

@Test(timeout = 5000)

In the above case, it will terminate the test method in 5 seconds and the method will be marked as 'Failed'.

### 53. What is the use of testng.xml file?

Ans. testng.xml file is used for configuring the whole test suite. In testng.xml file we can create test suite, create test groups, mark tests for parallel execution, add listeners and pass parameters to test scripts. Later this testng.xml file can be used for triggering the test suite.

### 54. What is the use of @Listener annotation in TestNG?

TestNG listeners are used to configure reports and logging. One of the most widely used listeners in TestNG is ITestListener interface. It has methods like onTestStart, onTestSuccess, onTestFailure, onTestSkipped etc. We should implement this interface creating a listener class of our own. Next, we should add the listeners annotation (@Listeners) in the Class which was created.

### 55. How to run a group of test cases using TestNG?

TestNG allows you to perform sophisticated groupings of test methods. Not only can you declare that methods belong to groups, but you can also specify groups that contain other groups. Then TestNG can be invoked and asked to include a certain set of groups (or regular expressions) while excluding another set. This gives you maximum flexibility in how you partition your tests and doesn't require you to recompile anything if you want to run two different sets of tests back to back.

## 56. How to create and run TestNG.xml?

In TestNG framework, we need to create TestNG XML file to create and handle multiple test classes. We do configure our test run, set test dependency, include or exclude any test, method, class or package and set priority etc in the XML file.

## 57. What are commonly used TestNG annotations?

The commonly used TestNG annotations are-

@Test- @Test annotation marks a method as Test method.

@BeforeSuite- The annotated method will run only once before all tests in this suite have run.

@AfterSuite-The annotated method will run only once after all tests in this suite have run.

@BeforeClass-The annotated method will run only once before the first test method in the current class is invoked.

@AfterClass-The annotated method will run only once after all the test methods in the current class have been run.

@BeforeTest-The annotated method will run before any test method belonging to the classes inside the <test> tag is run.

@AfterTest-The annotated method will run after all the test methods belonging to the classes inside the <test> tag have run.

### 58. Why to use TestNG with Selenium RC?

If you want full automation against different server and client platforms, you need a way to invoke the tests from a command line process, reports that tells you what happened and flexibility in how you create your test suites. TestNG gives that flexibility.

### 59. What is the difference Between Web Driver Listeners and Testers Listeners?

TestNG and Web Drive Listener are various interfaces to implement and invite them. They both change their behavior. You can use questions that are aware of. FireFoxDriver Drive = New FireFoxDriver (); This URL provides a comprehensive list of listeners and their interfaces.

### 60. From your test script how you can create html test report?

To create html test report there are three ways

TestNG: Using inbuilt default.html to get the HTML report. Also, XLST reports from ANT, Selenium, TestNG combination

JUnit: With the help of ANT

Using our own customized reports using XSL jar for converting XML content to HTML

### 61. What is Listener in Selenium WebDriver?

In Selenium WebDriver, Listeners "listen" to the event defined in the selenium script and behave accordingly. It allows customizing TestNG reports or logs. There are two main listeners i.e. WebDriver Listeners and TestNG Listeners.

### 62. Can we use Selenium RC to drive tests on two different browsers on one operating system without Selenium Grid?

Yes, it is possible when you are not using JAVA testing framework. Instead of using Java testing framework if you are using java client driver of selenium then TestNG allows you to do this. By using "parallel=test" attribute you can set tests to be executed in parallel and can define two different tests, each using different browser.

### 63. In Selenium what are Breakpoints and Start points?

Breakpoints: When you implement a breakpoint in your code, the execution will stop right there. This helps you to verify that your code is working as expected.

Startpoints: It indicates the point from where the execution should begin. Startpoint can be used when you want to run the test script from the middle of the code or a breakpoint.

### 64. What are the types of waits available in WebDriver?

There are two types of waits available in WebDriver

Implicit Wait

Explicit Wait

Implicit Wait: Implicit waits are used to provide a default waiting time (say 10 seconds) between each consecutive test step/command across the entire test script. Thus, subsequent test step would only execute when the 10 seconds have elapsed after executing the previous test step/command.

Explicit Wait: Explicit waits are used to halt the execution till the time a condition is met, or the maximum time has elapsed. Unlike Implicit waits, explicit waits are applied for an instance only.

## 65. Who developed Selenium Testing Tool?

Jason Huggins and team developed this tool in 2004 when they were working for Thought work (IT outsourcing company). They created this tool for the testing of an internal time & expenses application written in (python).

## 66. What are the JUnits annotation linked with Selenium?

The JUnits annotation linked with Selenium are

@Before public void method() – It will perform the method () before each test, this method can prepare the test

@Test public void method() – Annotations @Test identifies that this method is a test method environment

@After public void method()- To execute a method before this annotation is used, test method must start with test@Before

## 67. How is Selenium different from commercial browser automation tools?

Selenium is a library which is available in many languages i.e. java, C#, python, ruby, php etc. while most commercial tools are limited in their capabilities of being able to use just one language. More over many of those tools have their own proprietary language which is of little use outside the domain of those tools. Most commercial tools focus on record and replay while Selenium emphasis on using Selenium IDE (Selenium record and replay) tool only to get acquainted with Selenium working and then move on to more mature Selenium libraries like Remote control (Selenium 1.0) and Web Driver (Selenium 2.o).

Though most commercial tools have built-in capabilities of test reporting, error recovery mechanisms and Selenium does not provide any such features by default. But given the rich set of languages available with Selenium, it very easy to emulate such features.

## 68. What are the four components of selenium?

There are four Components:

1)Selenium WebDriver

2)Selenium Grid

3)Selenium Remote Control (Selenium RC)

4)Selenium Integrated Development Environment (Selenium IDE)

## 69. What are the types of Locater in WebDriver?

- id

- name

- classname

- css selector

- xpath: Xpath is unique locater in selenium to recognize an object based on tagname.

- LinkText: a link having some outer text ie., linktext.

- PartialLinktext: link text with unique characters.

- TagName: tagName generally we use for to identify a group of objects.

## 70. What is XPath?

XPath or XML path is a query language for selecting nodes from XML documents. XPath is one of the locators supported by selenium web driver.

Using XPath, we could navigate through elements and attributes in an XML document to locate web elements such as textbox, button, checkbox, Image etc., in a web page.

## 71. What are various types of XPath?

Types of XPath are

-Absolute XPath

-Relative XPath

## 72. What is an absolute XPath?

An absolute XPath is a way of locating an element using an XML expression beginning from root node i.e. html node in case of web pages. The main disadvantage of absolute XPath is that even with slightest change in the UI or any element the whole absolute XPath fails.

**73. What is a relative XPath?**

A relative XPath is a way of locating an element using an XML expression beginning from anywhere in the HTML document. There are different ways of creating relative XPaths which are used for creating robust XPaths (unaffected by changes in other UI elements).

Example - //input[@id='username']

**74. What is the difference between "/" and "//" in XPath?**

Single Slash "/" – Single slash is used to create XPath with absolute path i.e. the XPath would be created to start selection from the document node/start node.

Double Slash "//" – Double slash is used to create XPath with relative path i.e. the XPath would be created to start selection from anywhere within the document.

**75. How to find an element using XPath with 'and' operator?**

driver.findElement(By.xpath("//tagname[@attribute1='value1' and @attribute2='value2']"))  this XPath will select the element with attribute1 with value1 and attribute2 with value2

**76. How to find XPath using index?**

//tagname[number]

Ex: driver.findElement(By.xpath("//tr[2]/td[2]"))

This will select second td element in second row(tr)

)

### 77. How can we locate an element by the only partially matching its attributes value in the Xpath?

Using contains () method we can locate an element by the partially matching its attribute's value. This is particularly helpful in the scenarios like where the attributes have dynamic values with the certain constant part.

XPath expression = //*[contains(@name,'user')]

The above that statement will match the all the values of name attribute to containing the word 'user' in them.

### 78. How can we move to the parent of an element using XPath?

Using '..' expression in XPath we can move to the parent of an element.

### 79. When you use these locators, ID, Name, XPath, Or CSS Selector?

ID & Name locators will be used when there are unique identifiers & unique names available on the web page.

XPath is used when there are no preferred locators.

CSS Selector can be used for performance and when ID & Name locators are not unique.

## 80. What is Desired Capability?

The desired capability is a series of key/value pairs that stores the browser properties like browser name, browser version, the path of the browser driver in the system, etc. to determine the behavior of the browser at run time.

## 81. How Desired Capability is used in Selenium?

-It can be used to configure the driver instance of Selenium WebDriver.

-When you want to run the test cases on a different browser with different operating systems and versions.

## 82. How can you use Selenium to identify an object?

Use isElementPresent (String locator) to find an object using Selenium. It takes a locator as the argument and if found, returns a Boolean.

## 83. What is regular expressions? How you can use regular expressions in Selenium?

A regular expression is a special text string used for describing a search pattern. In Selenium IDE regular expression can be used with the keyword- regexp: as a prefix to the value and patterns needs to be included for the expected values.

## 84. What are the testing types that can be supported by Selenium?

Selenium supports the following types of testing:

Functional Testing

Regression Testing

### 85. What are the Programming Languages supported by Selenium WebDriver?

Java

C#

Python

Ruby

Perl

PHP

### 86. What are Selenium components?

Selenium is a suite of tools for automated web testing.

It is composed of:

Selenium IDE (Integrated Development Environment). It is a tool for recording and playing back. It is a Firefox plugin.

WebDriver and RC. It provides the APIs for a variety of languages like Java, .NET, PHP, etc. They work with most of the browsers.

Grid: It can distribute tests on multiple machines so that test can be run parallel which helps cutting down the time required for running test suites in the browser.

### 87. What is assert in Selenium?

Asserts are used to perform validations in the test scripts.

### 88. Name various types of asserts in selenium?

There are two types of Asserts:

Hard Assert

Soft Assert

## 89. What are Hard Assert and Soft Assert in Selenium?

Hard assert: – When an assert fails the test script stops execution unless handled in some form. We call general assert as Hard Assert

It marks method as fail if assert condition gets failed and the remaining statements inside the method will be aborted.

Soft assert: -Soft Assert does not throw an exception when an assert fails and would continue with the next step after the assert statement.

## 90. What is the difference between verify and assert commands?

Assert:  Assert allows to check whether an element is on the page or not. The test will stop on the step failed, if the asserted element is not available. In other words, the test will have terminated at the point where check fails.

Verify: Verify command will check whether the element is on the page, if it is not then the test will carry on executing.  In verification, all the commands are going to run guaranteed even if any of test fails.

## 91. Name different exceptions Selenium web drivers throw?

The different exceptions Selenium web drivers throw are

WebDriverException

NoAlertPresentException

NoSuchWindowException

NoSuchElementException

TimeoutException

## 92. What is Continuous Integration?

Continuous Integration (CI) is a development practice that requires developers to integrate code into a shared repository several times a day. Each check-in is then verified by an automated build, allowing teams to detect problems early. By integrating regularly, you can detect errors quickly, and locate them more easily.

## 93. What are the benefits of CI?

Continuous Integration has multiple benefits as below:

Increase visibility enabling greater communication

Catch issues early and nip them in the bud

Spend less time debugging and more time adding features

Build a solid foundation

Stop waiting to find out if your code's going to work

Reduce integration problems allowing you to deliver software more rapidly

## 94. Name some of the continuous integration tools?

Some of the continuous integration tools are Jenkins, TeamCity, Bamboo, Travis, Circle Ci, Bitbucket.

## 95. What is the difference between MaxSessions Vs. MaxInstances properties in selenium grid?

MaxInstances is the no. of browser instances of the same version of the browser that can run on the remote machine.

MaxSession says how many browsers, independent of the type & version, can run in parallel on the remote machine.

## 96. Explain how you can insert a break point in Selenium IDE?

In Selenium IDE to insert a break point

Select "Toggle break point" by right click on the command in Selenium IDE

Press "B" on the keyboard and select the command in Selenium IDE

Multiple break points can be set in Selenium IDE

From Selenium IDE how you can execute a single line?

From Selenium IDE single line command can be executed in two ways

Select "Execute this command" by right clicking on the command in Selenium IDE

Press "X" key on the keyboard after selecting the command in Selenium IDE

### 97. What format does the source view shows scripts in Selenium IDE?

In Selenium IDE source view shows your script in XML format

### 98. Explain how you can insert a start point in Selenium IDE?

In two ways selenium IDE can be set

Press "S" key on the keyboard and select the command in Selenium IDE

In Selenium IDE right click on the command and the select "Set / Clear Start Point"

### 99. What if you have written your own element locator and how would you test it?

To test the locator, one can use "Find Button" of Selenium IDE, as you click on it, you would see on screen an element being highlighted provided your element locator is right or else an error message will be displayed

### 100. How to debug tests using Selenium IDE?

Insert a break point from the location from where you want to execute test step by step

Run the test case

At the given break point execution will be paused

To continue with the next statement, click on the blue button

Click on the "Run" button to continue executing all the commands at a time

## 101. List some scenarios which we cannot automate using Selenium WebDriver?

1. Bitmap comparison is not possible using Selenium WebDriver

2. Automating Captcha is not possible using Selenium WebDriver

3. Bar code cannot read using Selenium WebDriver

## 102. What is heightened privileges browsers?

The purpose of heightened privileges is like Proxy Injection, allows websites to do something that are not commonly permitted.  The key difference is that the browsers are launched in a special mode called heightened privileges.  By using these browser modes, Selenium core can open the AUT directly and read/write its content without passing the whole AUT through the Selenium RC server.

## 103. What is Selenese?

Selenese is a selenium set of command which are used for running the test

## 104. Name various the types of Selenese?

There are three types of Selenese

Actions: It is used for performing the operations and interactions with the target elements

Assertions: It is used as a check point

Accessors: It is used for storing the values in a variable

## 105. What is core extension?

If you want to "extend" the default functionality provided by Selenium Function Library, you can create a Core Extension. They are also called "User Extension".

## 106. What are the different keyboard operations that can be performed in selenium?

The different keyboard operations that can be performed in selenium are-

.sendKeys("sequence of characters") - Used for passing character sequence to an input or textbox element.

.pressKey("non-text keys") - Used for keys like control, function keys etc. that are non-text.

.releaseKey("non-text keys") - Used in conjunction with keypress event to simulate releasing a key from keyboard event.

## 107. Explain how you can handle colors in web driver?

To handle colors in web driver you can use

Use getCssValue(arg) function to get the colors by sending 'color' string as an argument

## 108. How will you verify the specific position of a web element?

You can use verifyElementPositionLeft & verifyElementPositionTop. It does a pixel comparison of

the position of the element from the Left and Top of page respectively.

## 109.How can you handle network latency in Selenium?

Use driver.manage.pageloadingtime for network latency.

## 110. What is @CacheLookup annotation in PageFactory?

PageFactory annotation @CacheLookup is used to mark the WebElements once located so that the same instance in the DOM can always be used. CacheLookup attribute can be used to instruct the InitElements() method to cache the element once its located and so that it will not be searched over and over again.

## 111. How can we handle Web-based pop-up?

There are four methods of the effective Web-based pop-up handling:

String getText()method returns the text displayed on the alert box

void accept () method clicks on the "Ok" button as soon as the pop-up window appears

void dismiss () method clicks on the "Cancel" button as soon as the pop-up window appears

void sendKeys (String stringToSend) method enters the specified string pattern into the alert box

## 112. Explain what are the JUnits annotation linked with Selenium?

The JUnits annotation linked with Selenium are

@Before public void method() – It will perform the method () before each test, this method can prepare the test

@Test public void method() – Annotations @Test identifies that this method is a test method environment

@After public void method()- To execute a method before this annotation is used, test method must start with test@Before

### 113. How to use click method with and without parameter?

click(): This method clicks at the current mouse location

click(WebElement onElement):clicks the mouse on the specified element.

### 114. What is synchronization?

Matching the automation tool speed with application speed is called synchronization.

### 115.Which WebDriver implementation claims to be the fastest?

The fastest implementation of WebDriver is the HTMLUnitDriver. It is because the HTMLUnitDriver does not execute tests in the browser.

### 116.What are the Operating Systems supported by Selenium WebDriver?

Windows

Linux

Apple

## 117.What are the Open-source Frameworks supported by Selenium WebDriver?

JUnit

TestNG

## 118. Can WebDriver test Mobile applications?

WebDriver cannot test Mobile applications. WebDriver is a web-based testing tool, therefore applications on the mobile browsers can be tested.

## 119. How to launch the browser using WebDriver?

The following syntax can be used to launch Browser:

WebDriver driver = new FirefoxDriver();

WebDriver driver = new ChromeDriver();

WebDriver driver = new InternetExplorerDriver();

## 120. FirefoxDriver is a Class or an Interface?

FirefoxDriver is a Java class, and it implements the WebDriver interface.

## 121. How you can use "submit" a form using Selenium?

You can use "submit" method on element to submit form-

element. submit ();

Alternatively, you can use click method on the element which does form submission.

## 122. Explain what is the difference between find elements () and find element ()?

findelement () :-It finds the first element within the current page using the given "locating mechanism".  It returns a single WebElement

findelements (): - Using the given "locating mechanism" find all the elements within the current page.  It returns a list of web elements.

## 123. What is the difference between driver.Close() and driver.quit() command?

Close () - It is used to close the browser or page currently which is having the focus.

Quit() - It is used to shut down the web driver instance or destroy the web driver instance (Close all the windows).

## 124. Explain using Webdriver how you can perform double click?

You can perform double click by using

Syntax- Actions act = new Actions (driver);

act. DoubleClick(webelement);

## 125. How will you use Selenium to upload a file?

File uploading action could be performed by using element.sendKeys("path of file") on the webElement of input tag and type file: < name="fileUpload" type="file" />

## 126. How to handle windows-based Alerts/Pop-Ups in Selenium?

Handling a window-based pop-up is not straight-forward. Selenium only supports web applications and doesn't provide a way to automate Windows-based applications. However, the following approaches can help.

Use the Robot class (Java-based) utility to simulate the keyboard and mouse actions. That's how you can handle the window-based pop.

The KeyPress and KeyRelease methods simulate the user pressing and releasing a specific key on the keyboard.

### 127.What is Fluent Wait in Selenium WebDriver?

FluentWait can define the maximum amount of time to wait for a specific condition and frequency with which to check the condition before throwing an "ElementNotVisibleException" exception.

### 128.When AutoIT is used?

AutoIT is used to handle window GUI and non-HTML popups in the application.

### 129. Explain how you can login into any site if it's showing any authentication popup for password and username?

Pass the username and password with URL

Syntax-http://username:password@url

### 130. How to inspect the web element attributes to use them in different locators?

Using Firebug or developer tools we can inspect the specific web elements.

Firebug is a plugin of Firefox that provides various development tools for debugging applications. From automation perspective, firebug is used specifically for inspecting web-elements to use their attributes like id, class, name etc. in different locators.

### 131. How to switch between multiple windows in selenium?

Selenium has driver.getWindowHandles() and driver.switchTo().window("{windowHandleName}") commands to work with multiple windows. The getWindowHandles() command returns a list of ids corresponding to each window and on passing a window handle to driver.switchTo().window("{windowHandleName}") command we can switch control/focus to that window.

### 132. How to fetch the current page URL in selenium?

Using getCurrentURL() command we can fetch the current page URL-

driver.getCurrentUrl();

### 133. How can we check if an element is getting displayed on a web page?

Using isDisplayed() method we can check if an element is getting displayed on a web page.

driver.findElement(By locator).isDisplayed();

### 134. How can we check if an element is enabled for interaction on a web page?

Using isEnabled() method we can check if an element is enabled or not.

driver.findElement(By locator).isEnabled();

### 135. How will you handle working with multiple windows in Selenium?

We can use the command select Window to switch between windows. This command uses the title of Windows to identify which window to switch.

### 136. Why do we need Session Handling?

During test execution, the Selenium WebDriver must interact with the browser all the time to execute given commands. At the time of execution, it is also possible that, before current execution completes, someone else starts execution of another script, in the same machine and in the same type of browser. In such situation, we need a mechanism by which our two different executions should not overlap with each other. This can be done using session handling in Selenium.

### 137. Explain how you can find broken images in a page using Selenium Web driver?

To find the broken images in a page using Selenium web driver is

Get Xpath and get all the links in the page using tag name

In the page click on each link

Look for 404/500 in the target page title

### 138. What is Robot API?

Robot API is used to control keyboard or mouse to interact with OS windows like Download pop-up, Alerts, Print Pop-ups, etc. or native Operation System applications like Notepad, Skype, Calculator, etc.

### 139. How to fetch title of the page in selenium?

Using driver.getTitle() method we can fetch the page title in selenium. This method returns a string containing the title of the webpage.

### 140. How to delete cookies in selenium?

Using deleteAllCookies() method cookies can be deleted.

driver.manage().deleteAllCookies();

### 141. How can you retrieve the message in an alert box?

You can use the storeAlert command which will fetch the message of the alert pop up and store it in a variable.

### 142. How do you identify an object using selenium?

To identify an object using Selenium you can use

isElementPresent (String locator)

isElementPresent takes a locator as the argument and if found returns a Boolean

### 143. To generate pdf reports mention what Java API is required?

To generate pdf reports, you need Java API IText.

### 144. Can Selenium handle windows-based pop up?

Selenium is an automation testing tool which supports only web application testing, that means, it doesn't support testing of windows-based applications. However, Selenium alone can't help the situation but along with some third-party intervention, this problem can be overcome. There are several third-party tools available for handling window-based pop ups along with the selenium like AutoIT, Robot class etc.

### 145. How to assert title of the web page?

assertTrue ("The title of the window is incorrect.", driver. getTitle ().equals("Title of the page"));

### 146. How can I read test data from excels?

Test data can efficiently be read from excel using JXL or POI API

### 147.What verification points are available with Selenium?

There are largely three type of verification points available with selenium:

– Check for page title

– Check for certain text

– Check for certain element (textbox, drop down, table etc)

### 148. Do you know a way to refresh browser by using Selenium?

The list of commands to refresh a page in Selenium:

navigate().refresh()

getCurrentUrl()

navigate().to(driver.getCurrentUrl())

sendKeys(Keys.F5)

## 149. How can we handle web-based pop up?

WebDriver offers the users with a very efficient way to handle these pop-ups using Alert interface. There are the four methods that we would be using along with the Alert interface.

void dismiss() – The accept() method clicks on the "Cancel" button as soon as the pop-up window appears.

void accept() – The accept() method clicks on the "Ok" button as soon as the pop-up window appears.

String getText() – The getText() method returns the text displayed on the alert box.

void sendKeys(String stringToSend) – The sendKeys() method enters the specified string pattern into the alert box.

## 150. What is same origin policy? How you can avoid same origin policy?

The "Same Origin Policy" is introduced for security reason, and it ensures that content of your site will never be accessible by a script from another site.  As per the policy, any code loaded within the browser can only operate within that website's domain.

To avoid "Same Origin Policy" proxy injection method is used, in proxy injection mode the Selenium Server acts as a client configured HTTP proxy, which sits between the browser and application under test and then masks the AUT under a fictional URL.

### 151. What is IntelliJ?

IntelliJ is an IDE that helps you to write better and faster code for Selenium. IntelliJ can be used in the option to Java bean and Eclipse.

### 152. What is elementary process?

Software applications are made up of several elementary processes. There are two types of elementary processes: Dynamic elementary Process: The dynamic elementary involves process of moving data from one location to another. The location can be either within the application or outside it. Static elementary Process: It involves maintaining the data of the application.

### 153. What are the two modes of views in Selenium IDE?

Selenium IDE can be opened either in side bar (View > Side bar > Selenium IDE) or as a pop up window (Tools > Selenium IDE). While using Selenium IDE in browser side bar it cannot record user operations in a pop up window opened by application.

### 154. What is Selenium Accessors?

Accessors are those commands which allow the user to store certain values to a user-defined variable. These stored values can be later used to create assertions and verifications.

### 155. What is the difference between setSpeed() and sleep() methods?

Both will delay the speed of execution.

SetSpeed () : For specific amount of time it will stop the execution for every selenium command.

-It takes a single argument in integer format

Ex: selenium.setSpeed("3000")- It will wait for 3 seconds

-Runs each command after setSpeed() delay by the number of milliseconds mentioned in set Speed

Thread.sleep () : It will stop the current (java) thread for the specified period of time.

-It takes a single argument in integer format

Ex: thread.sleep(3000)- It will wait for 3 seconds

-It waits only once at the command given at sleep

### 156. What are the benefits of Selenium over WebDriver?

- Supports many browsers and many languages, WebDriver needs native implementations for each new language/browser combo.

- Very mature and complete API

- supports JavaScript alerts and performs better

### 157. What are the benefits of WebDriver compared to Selenium?

- Native automation faster and a little less prone to error and browser configuration

- Does not require Selenium-RC Server to be running

- Access to headless HTML unit can allow tests to run very fast

- Great APIs

### 158. Is it possible to control the speed and pause test execution in Selenium IDE?

Selenium IDE provides a slider with Slow and Fast pointers to control the speed of execution.

### 159. What is soft assertion in Selenium?

Soft Assertions are customized error handlers provided by TestNG. Soft Assertions do not throw exceptions when assertion fails, and they simply continue to the next test step. They are commonly used when we want to perform multiple assertions.

### 160. How can you mark a test case as failed by using soft assertion?

To mark a test as failed with soft assertions, call assertAll() method at the end of the test.

### 161. Explain what does @Test(invocationCount=?) and @Test(threadPoolSize=?) indicate.?

@Test(invocationCount=?) is a parameter that indicates the number of times this method should be invoked.

@Test(threadPoolSize=?) is used for executing suites in parallel. Each suite can be run in a separate thread.

### 162. How many parameters do you have to meet for Selenium to pass a test?

There are four conditions (parameters) for Selenium to pass a test. These are as follows: URL, host, browser and port number.

### 163. How would you find broken links on a webpage with the Webdriver?

To do so, you'll have to use the driver.get() function. You would have to imply the tags of <a>, and for each <a> that shows up, simply run the before mentioned function as a test. Any links that don't come back as "200 – OK" are broken.

### 164. Which WebDriver API is the fastest, and why?

It is none other than the HTMLUnitDriver, which is faster than all of its counter parts. The technical reason is that the HTMLUnitDriver doesn't execute in the browser. It employs a simple HTTP request-response mechanism for test case execution. This method is far quicker than starting a browser to carry out test execution.

### 165. What is the difference between maxsessions vs. maxinstances properties of Selenium Grid?

MaxInstances: It is the no. of browser instances (of the same versions) that can run on the remote machine.

MaxSession: It dictates how many browsers (independent of the type & version) can run concurrently on the remote machine. It supersedes the "MaxInstances" setting.

### 166. Which is the super interface of Selenium Web Driver?

Th SearchContext acts as the super interface for the Web Driver.

It is the external interface which has only two methods: findElement() and findElements()

### 167. Why do we create a reference variable of type webdriver, not the actual browser type?

It is because we could use the same Webdriver variable to hold the object of any browser, such as the ChromeDriver, IEDriver, or SafariDriver, etc.

# We follow this approach as it can work with any browser instance.

WebDriver driver = new FirefoxDriver();

# This approach is right too but will work only the Firefox.

FirefoxDriver driver = new FirefoxDriver();

### 168. Is it mandatory to prefix the url with http or https while calling the web driver's Get() method?

Yes, if the URL doesn't contain the HTTP prefix, then the program will throw an exception.

Hence, it is mandatory to pass the HTTP or HTTPS protocol while calling the web driver's get() method.

## 169. What is the other method which gives the same effect as we get from the web driver's get()?

Selenium provides the "navigate.to(link)" method. It does the same thing as we achieve from the get() call.

## 170. What is the principal difference between "GET" and "NAVIGATE" methods?

Get method makes a page to load or extracts its source or parse the full text. On the contrary, the navigate method tracks the history and can perform operations like refresh, back, and forward.

For example – We like to move forward, execute some functionality and then move back to the home page.

We can achieve this by calling the Selenium's navigate () API.

The driver.get() method waits until the page finish loading.

The driver.navigate() will only redirect and return immediately.

## 171. What is the difference between web driver's getwindowhandle() and getwindowhandles() methods?

webdriver.getWindowHandle() – It gets the handle of the active web page.

webdriver.getWindowHandles() – It gets the list of handles for all the pages opened at a time.

## 172. How to handle multiple Popup windows in Selenium?

Selenium provides the getWindowHandles() method, which returns the handles for all open popups.

We can store them into a <String> variable and convert it into an array.

After that, we can traverse the array and navigate to a specific window by using the below code.

driver.switchTo().window(ArrayIndex);

### 173. What are user extensions, and how do you create them?

User extensions are a set of functions written in JavaScript. They are present in a separate known as the extension file. Selenium IDE or Selenium RC access it to activate the extensions.

Selenium's core has a JavaScript codebase. So, you can also use it to create the extension.

### 174. Name the mobile device which Selenium supports?

1- It supports Safari browser via a third-party driver. It is experimental and comes with limited functionality.

2- It provides an Android driver to run tests on its native mobile browser.

### 175. What type of tests Selenium can run?

1- You can use Selenium for the functional, regression, and load testing of the web-based applications.

2- You can employ this tool for doing the post-release validation.

3- Integrate it with the continuous integration tools like Jenkins, Hudson, QuickBuild or CruiseControl.

### 176. What is Behavior Driven Development (BDD) Framework?

BDD follows most of the principles of Test-Driven Development Framework but replaces its unit-centric approach with a domain-centric design.

It intends to bring in inputs not only from the Dev or QA but an array of stakeholders such as Product Owners, Technical Support, Managers, and Customers.

The goal is to identify and automate appropriate tests that reflect the behavior sought by the principal stakeholders.

### 177. Name any 3 popular BDD testing tools.

1. Cucumber

2. JBehave

3. Specflow

### 178. What is Cucumber?

Cucumber is an automation testing framework used to test the software applications easily without any programming skills. This is an open source tool and supports plain English language specifications for the testing requirements.

### 179. What language is used by Cucumber?

Gherkin is the language that is used by the Cucumber tool. It is a simple English representation of the application behavior. Gherkin language uses several keywords to describe the behavior of applications such as Feature, Scenario, Scenario Outline, Given, When, Then, etc.

## 180. What are the major advantages of the Cucumber?

Below are the advantages of the Cucumber:

-Cucumber is an open-source tool.

-Plain Text representation makes it easier for non-technical users to understand the scenarios.

-It bridges the communication gap between various project stakeholders such as Business Analysts, Developers, and Quality Assurance personnel.

-Automation test cases developed using the Cucumber tool are easier to maintain and understand as well.

-Easy to integrate with other tools such as Selenium and Capybara.

## 181. What are the two files required to run a cucumber test?

-Feature file

-Step Definition file

## 182. What is a feature in cucumber?

A feature can be defined as a unit or functionality or part of a project which is an independent functionality of the project. A feature contains a group of scenarios which are to be tested as a feature. There are two parts in a feature in Cucumber tool which is called feature files having scenarios in it and the feature files containing automation steps or procedure to be executed.

### 183. What is a feature file in cucumber?

Feature file is an entry point of Cucumber execution. Cucumber scenarios are written inside the feature file using a plain-text language called Gherkin. It can contain a scenario or multiple scenarios. To add a feature file in the project, the scenario or feature to be automated must be identified first, then feature file is added and test runner class is created.

### 184. What is the file extension of feature file?

.feature is the extension of feature file. Example, "Test.feature" is a feature file name.

### 185. What is the language used to write a scenario in feature file?

Gherkin is a plain-text language used to write cucumber scenario in the feature file. Gherkin is a business readable, domain-specific language used to describe the behavior of software application from user's perspective so that its easy for non-programmers to read and collaborate.

### 186. What does a feature file contain?

A feature file in cucumber specifies parameters and conditions for executing the test code. It can combine any of the following.

1. A feature.

2. A user scenario.

3. The scenario outline.

4. A <Given> clause.

5. A <When> clause.

6. A <Then> clause.

## 187. How to integrate Cucumber with Selenium Web driver?

Cucumber is a testing framework to run acceptance test cases. It creates scripts using the BDD approach.

To start Cucumber with Selenium, first, you require creating a Maven project in Eclipse.

In the Maven's POM file, you add the Cucumber dependency which brings the support of annotations like the <Given>, <When>, and <Then> and many other.

Similarly, you can introduce the Selenium dependency into the above project. Alternatively, you can download the latest version of Selenium standalone jar from their website. And then, add to your project as an external jar file.

## 188. What is a profile in cucumber?

A Cucumber profiles is created to run a set of features and step definitions.

## 189. What are cucumber tags? And why do we use them?

Cucumber tags help in filtering the scenarios. We can tag the scenarios and then run them based on tags. We can add tags to scenarios with the <@> symbol.

We can use the following command to run a cucumber tagged scenario.

cucumber features -t @<tag_name>

## 190. What is a Step definition file?

A step definition is the actual code implementation of the feature, mentioned in the feature file.

## 191. What are Cucumber Hooks?

Cucumber supports hooks, which are blocks of code that run before or after each scenario. Cucumber Hooks allows us to better manage the code workflow and helps us to reduce the code redundancy.

## 192. What are Before, After, Beforestep and Afterstep Hooks?

Before: execute before the feature file execution

After: executes after the feature file execution

BeforeStep: executes before each step execution

AfterStep: executes after each step execution

## 193. What are the steps to generate a report in Cucumber?

When we execute Cucumber Scenarios, it automatically generates an output in the eclipse console. There is a default behavior associated with that output and we can also configure that output as per our needs.

We run the following command to produce HTML reports.

cucumber <featurename>.feature --format html --out report.html --format pretty

### 194. What is Scenario Outline in feature file?

Scenario outline is a way of parameterization of scenarios. This is ideally used when the same scenario needs to be executed for multiple sets of data, however, the test steps remain the same. Multiple sets of test data are provided by using 'Examples' in a tabular structure separated by pipes (| |)

### 195. What is the difference between Given, When, Then steps in feature file?

*Given* defines the context of the scenario

*When* defines the actions of the scenario

*Then* defines the outcome of the scenario

### 196. Name any advanced framework design that can be used with Cucumber?

-Page Object Model

-Log4j

-Extent Reporting

-Dependency Injection (Example: Pico Container)

-Object Repository

### 197. What is the use of Background keyword in Cucumber?

Background keyword is used to group multiple given statements into a single group. This is generally used when the same set of given statements are repeated in each scenario of the feature file.

### 198. What is the purpose of the Cucumber Options tag?

Cucumber Options tag is used to provide a link between the feature files and step definition files. Each step of the feature file is mapped to a corresponding method on the step definition file.

Below is the syntax of Cucumber Options tag:

@CucumberOptions(features="Features",glue={"StepDefinition"})

### 199. What are the difference between Jbehave and Cucumber?

However, the Cucumber and Jbehave share the same perspective, but there are few key differences:

-Jbehave is Java-based and Cucumber is Ruby-based.

-Jbehave is story-driven whereas the Cucumber is feature-driven.

### 200.  Explain when to use Rspec and when to use Cucumber?

-Rspec is used for Unit Testing.

-Cucumber can be used for System and Integration Tests.

### 201. What software do you need to run cucumber in JAVA?

1. Eclipse or IntelliJ IDE

2. Gradle or Maven build tool

3. Junit or TestNG testing framework

4. Cucumber

5. Selenium (To automate browser)

### 202. What is a step definition in cucumber?

Step definition maps the test case steps in the feature files to code. It executes the steps on Application Under Test and checks the outcomes against expected results. In order to execute step definition, it must match the given component in a feature.

### 203. What is the name of the plugin that is used to integrate Eclipse with Cucumber?

Cucumber Natural Plugin is the plugin that is used to integrate Eclipse with Cucumber.

### 204. What is the use of the TestRunner class in Cucumber?

TestRunner class is used to provide the link between the feature file and step definition file. A TestRunner class is generally an empty class with no class definition.

### 205. What is the difference between test harness and test framework?

Test harness is specific and Test framework is generic. For example, a test harness will include the exact information of the test management tool down to the login IDs to be used. A test framework, on the other hand, will simply say that a test management tool will do the respective activities.

### 206. Are there any test harness tools?

Test harness includes tools like automation software, test management software, etc. However, there are no specific tools to implement a test harness. All or any tools can be a part of Test Harness: QTP, JUnit, HP ALM- all of them can be constituent tools of any Test Harness.

### 207. What are the JUnits annotation linked with Selenium?

The JUnits annotation linked with Selenium are

@Before public void method() – It will perform the method () before each test, this method can prepare the test

@Test public void method() – Annotations @Test identifies that this method is a test method environment

@After public void method()- To execute a method before this annotation is used, test method must start with test@Before

■■■■■■■■■■■■■■■■■■■■■■■■■■■■■■■■■■■■■■■■■■■■■■■■■■

Please check this out:

Our other best-selling books are-

500+ Java & J2EE Interview Questions & Answers-Java & J2EE Programming

200+ Frequently Asked Interview Questions & Answers in iOS Development

200 + Frequently Asked Interview Q & A in SQL, PL/SQL, Database Development & Administration

200+ Frequently Asked Interview Questions & Answers in Manual Testing

200+ Frequently Asked Interview Q & A in Python Programming

100+ Frequently Asked Interview Q & A in Robotic Process Automation (RPA)

100+ Frequently Asked Interview Q & A in Cyber Security

100+ Frequently Asked Interview Questions & Answers in Scala

100+ Frequently Asked Interview Q & A in Swift Programming

100+ Frequently Asked Interview Questions & Answers in Android Development

Frequently asked Interview Q & A in Java programming

Frequently Asked Interview Questions & Answers in J2EE

Frequently asked Interview Q & A in Angular JS

Frequently asked Interview Q & A in Database Testing

Frequently asked Interview Q & A in Mobile Testing

Frequently asked Interview Questions & Answers in JavaScript

Frequently Asked Interview Questions & Answers in HTML5

■■■■■■■■■■■■■■■■■■■■■■■■■■■■■■■■■■■■■■■■■■■■■■■■■